Broken Body

Chris Pitts

Silver Lining Books
Woking

First published by Silver Lining Books
30 Oriental Road, Woking, Surrey, GU22 7AW
in 2022

By the Same Author
The Caring Game

ISBN 978-0-9550053-5-0

www.pennantpublishing.co.uk

Chapter One

There's a place for us, somewhere a place for us.

In the cool of a summer's evening, somewhere in England, a man is walking down an old city back-street when suddenly, the crash of a cymbal and the twang of an electric guitar thunder their way out onto the lonely pavement. The doors of the old building shake as the Castle Hill fellowship starts its mid-week service. Ten doors down the road 'The Haven' residential home is preparing to serve out the 8 p.m. pre bed-time cup of tea and one digestive biscuit to its doomed, dying residents.

The man stops outside the fellowship hall for a moment and hears the amplified voice of Pastor John Peters coming over the P-A. "Alleluia, I feel miracles in the air tonight!" The people loudly respond "Praise God".

Confused, but slightly elated, the man walks on till he is level with the front window of 'The Haven'. He sees the helpless stagnant inmates being fed and watered by 'carers'. These young girls, wearing hospital blue uniforms, are talking about their experiences down at the local nightclub. This conversation is taking place while one of them is pushing a contraption with a spout on it into an old man's mouth! The lukewarm liquid gurgles and chokes its way down the aging resident's throat, where an eternal Hell on earth plays out its miserable tune, as in similar theatres all over England.

And in old England's 'green and pleasant land' this ritualistic human behaviour continues, day in day out, week in week out, year in year out. Jerusalem is never built, miracles are claimed that don't take place, the helpless get less than conveyer belt care, the old die comfortless! Young people are seduced into entering hysterical religious theatres that mock the founder of the Christian faith. Damaged people, broken people, reside in a church that is a broken body. The words of a Roman governor cry out down the years "What is Truth?" To which may be added: 'Where is Truth?'

This book is the account of how one man, the author, went from the dizzy heights of evangelical ecstasy all the way down to acute depression and alcohol dependency.

This rather dramatic introduction is an attempt to somehow give the reader an insight into the vexed, schizophrenic environment of those trapped in a world that is called 'Christian' but, in fact, is something far more sinister and questionable.

This is not an assault on all the wonderful, humble, open hearted people that carry out acts of sacrificial love and serve the Master, and are better disciples than I will ever hope to be. Many such good people are stagnating and frustrated trying to be faithful to their Lord inside the claustrophobic demonstrative fellowships mentioned above. We celebrate and thank God for their lives.

Before we continue, we must always make time to be ruthlessly honest and acknowledge that we cannot trust everything to memory, and yes, our memories are sometimes very selective. This does not mean however that the victims who claim that they were subjected to religious abuse should be treated as unreliable or worse, their claims subject to hyperbole. I have had forty years to consider what happened to my fellow travelers and me! I have meticulously gone over every step and examined what happened; however, why it happened and how it happened are difficult to explain. Going back over those years has not been an enjoyable process; it has stirred up ghosts and memories that I shadow box with daily.

There is now a growing weight of evidence that strongly suggests that within the Christian church, things can go and have gone desperately wrong. Many evangelical fellowships are at times very much out of control. This is an account of one man's experience among the evangelicals, but it must be remembered that there are an untold number of people out there damaged by exactly the very same experience. I ask my readers to keep an open mind and read this account to the end before they react.

Over the past thirty years the definition of what people call 'Church' has changed dramatically. Many different groups under the broad umbrella term of 'The Evangelicals' have led this change.

Liberal churchmen, like Stephen Parsons have broken ranks and felt the need to speak out. He has helped push these issues into the arena of public debate.

Stephen Parsons in his book 'Ungodly Fear' has documented case histories of people that have experienced religious abuse. He has focused mainly on the area of evangelical fundamentalism. He by no means criticizes all evangelical activity but like me he sees a great problem in the way that 'The gospel' has been applied.

Stephen Parsons up to this present time is the only minister I know of to have crossed the party line and shone a spotlight on these abused damaged people, and for that I am extremely thankful.

The advent of the house church movement during the late 60's through to the 80's has changed the way that church is viewed in this country. The concept of 'church' has now in many areas been replaced by the word 'fellowship'. These fellowships do not rely on a Priest who has had conventional theological training; they believe that people can be called by God to lead a fellowship. Of course the old established churches remain and some have taken on the style of the independent house churches. New denominations have appeared and built large buildings to accommodate their followers. All this has taken place under the broad understanding of evangelical activity. Most of these groups would say they follow the Protestant understanding of 'Reformed Theology'.

Trying to engage the leaders of these fellowships in a dialogue about why and how so many people have been damaged by attending these fellowships is almost impossible.

However, many conflicting opinions around this subject exist and perhaps this has not helped those who want an independent enquiry and an open discussion on ways forward.

So often, the top-down structures of church hierarchies gloss over this subject for the simple reason that cloistered academia cannot understand the vulnerable, uneducated, lower levels of the working class, people that are easy targets for fellowships that offer them prescriptive answers. I'm afraid that only those who have experienced this kind of helplessness (and abuse) within these horrific religious theatres can really know the full extent of the damage done. Unless the victims are somehow empowered to speak out then I'm afraid the usual top-down structures always fail for many reasons, the most common being just plain ignorance. Many of the victims are uneducated and would need advocacy support, however the advocates themselves would need to be truly informed and again I'm afraid the usual training courses on offer will be next to useless here.

When we come to the modern evangelical movement and attempt any open discussion on this subject, their reaction is to see these attempts as an attack on their 'doctrinal orthodoxy'. No monitoring of these contagious religious theatres is in place. This leaves a vacuum, a kind of no man's land, where the genuine seeker is left totally unprotected and abandoned in a quasi-spiritual circus that, at its best, is just plain shallow, and at its worse, extremely dangerous.

The poorly educated and illiterate will always fall prey to these seductive, flamboyant 'Church fellowships' because they offer prescriptive solutions to their dreadful problems. When 'healings' and 'miracles' in their workplace are promised and nothing happens, they are then left in a dis-empowered state and are expected to help themselves. This they obviously cannot do! One of the most tragic side effects of this is that the victims begin to blame themselves; they react by saying; 'I didn't have enough faith'!

I don't want to leave the impression that it is only the poorly educated that fall victims to these demonstrative rogue fellowships. I have come across highly educated people who have suffered years of torment, simply because they chose to believe in men (and man-made rules in relation to religious behaviour) rather than God. The mental torment and destruction of personality has left dreadful desolation in these victims that mere words will always fail to describe. Something has to be done - we have to start somewhere.

Chapter Two

'Don't follow leaders - watch the parking meters'

Within this vexed and complicated issue we must turn things on their head and view things from the other side. It seems to me that the problem of rogue fellowships must also be laid alongside the problem some have called 'cloistered academia'. This is evidenced in extremes of liberal theology, where we end up with an established church dishing out a dead ritual under the shroud of a scholarly critique, where an elevation of the human intellect takes place, which to all intents and purposes dismisses divine revelation.

For some reason, it often happens that victims of rogue evangelical fellowship abuse are sent to 'ministers of religion' for 'counseling.' These 'Ministers' are often out of their depth, and are themselves products of a woolly liberal environment. This does about as much good for these damaged people as it does looking for a snowflake in Dante's vision of hell. As stated above the only churchman really qualified to counsel these people is Stephen Parsons; he has somehow managed to get inside the nervous system of this vexed problem.

The comforts of a religious theatre where professional ministers partake of a career instead of vocation will always be structured to fail. It will fail all those genuine seekers who have sometimes given a lifetime of commitment to 'a place of worship'. It will fail because real love cannot exist against proud 'churchianity' indifference.

As the bells of religion continue to toll, the victims mount up and it seems painfully evident that no one involved wants to talk about this in any real, meaningful way.

It seems that a series of unbreakable cycles continue at an alarming rate. For instance, my experience of contemporary religion started with a demonstrative encounter with a group calling themselves 'The Navigators'. This was a well-organised evangelical group that targeted the intelligentsia of the day, particularly students. This group was very active during the late 1960's and early 70's.

The most incredible part of this story is that I was actually there in that place at that time. Let me explain: my best friend Bob had gone off to Warwick University in 1967 to study Physics. Bob and I had formed a strong friendship despite my illiteracy. We both attended a secondary modern school in Suffolk. Bob and I went to the same classroom each morning for the 'morning register of attendance'. In fact I sat directly behind his desk each morning. This was a bizarre schizophrenic experience. I could not read or write at the time and after 'Register,' I and my fellow 'Thickos' were hurried off to a cesspit of a place called 'Lower, Lower, Remove'. (I have written about my experience of illiteracy extensively in my book 'The Caring Game').

Bob was soon to be sent off to 'Grammar School'. However, we continued our friendship, sharing a common interest in the music medium of Folk/Blues.

When Bob left his native Suffolk to go to university I continued to work on the local farm. The curse of illiteracy leaves one in a vacuum where unskilled work is your only choice. I eventually decided to stay with Bob for a prolonged holiday. This was for me one of the strangest experiences of my life, the Fool on the Hill moves in with the physics student! With ways of hiding my illiteracy that only I knew at the time I made this absurd move.

I eventually found myself, in 1967, sleeping on the floor of his tiny room at E07 Roots Hall, Warwick University and scrounging money off Bob's grant! (No excuses offered).

Like a lot of people at that time we talked about the meaning of life, or what one wild 60's cat called 'The full Cosmic Event'! I was playing guitar and creating songs. My songs were committed to an ancient tape recorder. Sometimes Bob would write them out for me. None of Bob's friends guessed I was illiterate! I was a very good actor. I had started performing my songs at the university folk club and was amazed to find that I was getting good reviews in the university magazine. Alongside this I was sitting next to (as yet not famous) Germaine Greer in the university canteen! When I returned home I worked at the university of Essex as a toilet cleaner only visiting Bob on my days off. This was a frightening schizophrenic experience and I am still bewildered by it.

During the long summer of 1969 it became evident that the 1960's dream was coming to an end. We had enjoyed a time of great change and community spirit, but the worst side of human nature was destroying the dream in terms of personal ambition and status. A mass betrayal was taking place. We knew things were coming to an end and began to eagerly seek out other attempts at generous community.

The Navigators were involved in what I now understand to be a Christian 'Evangelical Outreach'. Universities were part of their target group. Eventually they got round to knocking on the door of EO7 Roots Hall.

What followed was a set of circumstances that were part accidental, part strategic, but most of all for us, very dangerous. The Navigators go all the way back to the 1930's, having their inception at Colorado Springs; becoming a very streamlined, evangelical disciple-seeking and training organization in the 60's and 70's.

As far as Bob and myself were concerned it meant that the 'Navs' wanted to convert us, smarten us up, and make us responsible members of society and not the skeptical drop–outs we were. We were invited to a Navigators evening meeting in Loughborough. A very nice man, Mr. Nicholson, drove us over there and back in his Morris 1100. On the way over the car broke down. Mr. Nicholson went to a phone box to ask Rob, the leader of the group at Loughborough, to 'pray that the car would get going again'. On coming out of the phone-box Mr. Nicholson slowly got into the driver's seat, bowed his head in prayer and turned the ignition key - the engine sprang into life! This made a lasting impression on two very young men.

That was a very memorable night. The Navigators had a special guest that evening; it was the actor James Fox. Mr. Fox had become very influenced by the Navigators; he gave quite a long talk on how he first met one of them in a hotel, where a member had 'gone away to be alone with God!'

As the evening wore on Bob and I were eventually introduced to an American Navigator/Evangelist - a Mr. Jack Blanche. What followed was an encounter with what can only fairly be described as one possible view of the New Testament scriptures! (The view of the modern evangelical movement?)

It would be true to say at this point that the

Navigators were good, well meaning people. Many were simply products of an inverted claustrophobic environment. Lateral thinking was unknown to them. They simply had no understanding of someone like me from the very bottom of the working class heap! They couldn't even try. They were like a polar bear trying to understand what it's like in a Turkish bath! One of the first things they did was to hand me a writing-pad and pencil; this sticks in my mind because it shows the narrow perspective of their worldview. As far as they were concerned 'everyone could read and write'.

It has to be chalked up as a sad reality that back in those days, the presentation of the Christian gospel by people like 'The Navigators,' had all the credibility of an academic vending machine.

Jack Blanche somehow managed to get Bob and myself into a small corner room - like the 'snug' in an old pub. He pulled out his Bible and began to read from the Book of Revelation chapter 3 verse twenty, "Behold I stand at the door and knock. If any man hear my voice and open the door, I will come in to him and sup with him and he with me," thus portraying Christ standing at the door of the human heart knocking, waiting to be invited in! After reading this he turned to Bob and myself, fixed us in the vacuum of his eyes, and in his deep American accent said 'Does this word lie'?

I looked at Bob, Bob looked at me, and I seem to have the memory that we murmured something positive... At our weakest point, when our psyche was about as unprotected as it could be, Bob Walker and Chris Pitts walked through a very dangerous portal.

I would like to make it clear at this point that I believe God can, and does, use anything and anyone to present His reality. However, what we experienced at that fateful meeting of the Navigators that night in late 1969 was, to quote an old Donovan song, "One man's opinion of moonlight". It's vitally important that we get this right; this is not about blame games, it's about victims, personality disorders and more, caused by one of the most common causes of religious abuse - *Selective use of scripture.*

For example, the very scripture that Mr. Blanche used that night, when taken in its historical setting, can and does have a very different message to the one presented to us. It is speaking of the church at Laodicea, a decadent materially rich smug body of people calling themselves Christ's church! Christ is in fact knocking at the door of His own church waiting to be invited in. What a different picture that suggests! We trusted implicitly that the nice, warm, good people we were among that night were presenting us with the truth. We had no understanding whatsoever that the 'Word of God' was subject to interpretation. To put a balance on this I think I must add: there is a legitimate way that Revelation 3:20 can be used in the context that Mr. Jack Blanche used that night. However, to put two very young people under the pressure to which we were exposed that night was, I think, very dangerous. This certainly was not an exposure to the uninhibited love of Christ. It was, in fact, putting us in a back-against-the-wall situation. Was it any wonder that later things went desperately wrong?

On returning to Essex I started to explore the churches in and around the area. The Pentecostal churches were at first quite terrifying places for me. Somehow I got sucked in to this demonstrative brain surgery. These were places that believed the miraculous gifts of healing that the early church experienced were still available to those of faith today. The environment was one of excited expectation. During all my years among Pentecostals I never witnessed one miracle, although I was programmed to say that I did! It became quite a natural thing to lie to people and to God. Is it any wonder that here and later at bible school with its emphasis on 'Shepherding,' that a madness invaded my being, the effects of which I still live in the shadow of today?

Doomed Youth's Swan Song

Although the relevance of this will possibly seem to the reader somewhat off track I feel I must give an account of a time long since past, long before Bob and I met the evangelicals. I do this because I think it important to show the freedoms we exchanged for the evangelical certainties and dogma that was traded off to us at our weakest point by well meaning people.

The wonderful experience of being young during those years of the 1960's was, for us, a taste of real freedom, perhaps the only one we were to have? It saddens me that those who were born after those years will never know that sacred time of youth 'when truth was being free'! There remains to this day a stale rank taste in my mouth when I reflect on what we lost, both in terms of knowledge and pure uninhibited enjoyment of life. Jesus spoke about those who 'load up heavy burdens on others but do not carry anything themselves'.

When I think of the time I wasted trying to 'Grow' inside stifling evangelical fellowships, and set that against the amount of work I could have put in fighting against social injustice, it makes me sick - very, very, sick. So those times of freedom need to be explained if I am to truly relate my experience and give real insight.

Back then there was an innocence and newness that made the air alive with hope. People were meeting up and sharing their money, their food, and their lives, in ways that had never happened before. The past generation was absolutely bewildered; however the establishment believed in 'give 'em a beating, knock some sense into them and make them useful members of society'. Being different in those days was dangerous; there was always a price to pay. The idea that we were all drug-taking lazy scroungers was, and is, quite simply a myth created by the media of the day. Back then St Ives in Cornwall 1967 was the place to be if you were on the seeking trails of youth! That summer gave us knowledge a sense of wonder that lived inside us and continues to do so today, something that religious programming could not, in the end, take away from us. These will be difficult lines to write because knowing something and explaining it to a third party is almost impossible.

Bob and I had been schooled on Bob Dylan's view of society. I remember the young Dylan singing: "The rules of the road have been lodged, its only people's games you got to dodge"

If we had managed to hold on to that we would have been safe! But we didn't. Try imagining a time when there was so much goodwill that trust became a perfectly natural reaction when meeting people. We lived in a world full of hope where all you needed was Love. The trouble started when we tried to take that further step to explore the ultimate answers to 'God the universe and everything'. What we didn't know, could not possibly know, was that there were thousands of individuals out there 'bent out of shape by society's pliers', ready to give us just that. Quite how Bob and I gave over our minds to an organization that claimed to represent the one true God is still causing a debate within my own thinking. However, the record shows that for some unfathomable reason we did. These days hardly an hour goes past when I don't think back to those times and fall into the bewildered rhythms of the mind. The sudden complete change from 'This is where you were' to 'This is where God wants you' is beyond my wit to explain.

Try imagining what it was like for someone from a working class socialist background suddenly arriving in 'God's Town,' where Mary Whitehouse was queen of all moral crusades and being a right wing reactionary was 'God's Will'? For some people the instant shedding of that skin simply drove them mad.

These victims are out there somewhere believing that the Christian faith is something that breaks you and destroys your life, or they are in some kind of hellish limbo, where they believe that God cannot reach them. Why is it so difficult for the modern evangelical to admit that these people exist and are so desperate for help. and when will they realize that they must first evangelize themselves and sort out this indescribable chaotic mess before they can have any real credibility? Exactly how people become cloned, indoctrinated into human vending machines, will involve an in-depth study. However, I am pleased to say that one lone figure in the Church of England has undertaken such a study. In his book Ungodly Fear (published by Lion), the Reverend Stephen Parsons takes on the whole subject of spiritual and religious abuse in ways that are way beyond any meager attempts that I could make. Reverend Parsons is a 'Modernist theologian' and at times some would regard him as on the outside of orthodoxy. The question that the modern evangelical leadership has to answer is this; Why has it taken a rank modernist in the Church of England to open his heart to the victims of abuse and the Evangelicals remain silent on this issue? You would have thought that the type of personality disorder that I and my fellow victims have shadow boxed with all these years would be given serious consideration; instead silence. Why?

My fellow victims and I were received into a movement that worshiped its own conclusions, received and welcomed by men and women that believed that God had approved of British capitalism; we were there to be modeled on an idol that would confirm their own prejudice. Oh yes, you can make an idol out of almost anything; that of course, includes making an idol out of the Bible.

Chapter Three

History According to Hal Lindsey

I met my wife Mary at St Ives Cornwall in 1967. By 1974 she had taught me to read and write. Mary sacrificed a great part of her life for me; words fail me here to describe the long grueling hours she gave to me. Somehow we got there and only God knows how! (A more detailed account of my struggle for literacy is given in my book 'The Caring Game'). I eventually achieved 'O Level' standard and passed an entrance exam to attend a 'Bible School'. I will talk about this later in chapter five.

One of the first things that happened to me after attaining literacy was that I started reading at an alarming rate. Soon however, I got hooked on religious literature especially books that dealt with Biblical prophecy. During the 1970's and 1980's there was a myriad of such books. I was an adult entering the world of literacy, but sadly to all intense and purposes I was actually like a little boy in short trousers in a sweet shop, not knowing that if you eat too much you will get sick! Discernment was as yet something I had not yet learned.

'Christian bookshops' were in the main stocking evangelical literature. At the time I was naive enough to believe that all Christians believed the same thing. I knew nothing about different interpretations of Holy Scripture. I now think of myself back then as a programmed receptacle blinkered and completely open to instruction. An extremely dangerous state to be in.

At that time there was a widespread belief among evangelical revivalists that the countdown to the second coming of Christ had begun with the establishment of the nation of Israel.

At this point in my life I retain a healthy agnosticism on the subject of biblical prophecy; however, back then I believed that people who wrote books knew what they were talking about. This mind set was linked to the presumptions that were linked to a 'born again experience'.

The major contributor on the subject of biblical Prophecy at the time was the American writer Hal Lindsey. Mr. Lindsey took on the vast subject of biblical eschatology in a way that was easy to understand. He wrote fluently and with dramatic effect. His readers went into millions overnight. I was one of those readers. Linked closely to this was the finely tuned cloning of evangelical personality and evangelical mentality, engineered by those who knew that they must first destroy the individual before their militarized society could flourish.

It was at this point, that the Evangelical brain police entered the space that once housed a free and uninhibited mind, a mind that was beginning to be at peace with itself. The violation and destruction of that young mind I refuse to describe here. I am now in the evening of my years; this book is for those victims who will follow me. I sincerely hope that this will help someone who is trapped inside a demonstrative fellowship where they are stagnating, blaming themselves for having a lack of faith. Yes, it is my sincere hope that you will see the brain police for what they are and move on.

The atmosphere back in those days was one of excited expectation. Books like Hal Lindsey's The Late Great Planet Earth gave out the hope of a better world just around the corner. Imagine being in a place where you whole-heartedly believe that a personal revelation has been delivered to you. First, I get the gift of literacy, then a modern day prophetic interpreter inducts you into the inner sanctuary of his prophetic insight. I believed with all my heart that the formally 'thick' Chris Pitts had finally arrived. If only I'd known at the time, that instead of arriving, I was departing on a ghost train, where animated figures moved on a landscape constructed to the precise dimensions of someone else's mind game.

I was soon to be immersed in the Hal Lindsey 'End-time Scenario'. I would speak the language of limited definition so recognizable in new age Christian societies today. Believing that the modern evangelicals were the only model of revelation that God was using in this present day, is it any wonder that I was so open to cloning? Here we have a vast complicated subject; how is it possible for someone from such a skeptical background to willingly allow the take-over of their mind, personality and powers of reason? Let me assure the reader that is exactly what happened and continues to happen today.

Back then Hal Lindsey was a one off, but today we have thousands of writers like Mr. Lindsey. Not only do they write books, they invade internet highways, accessing YouTube, the God channel, and every platform that welcomes them.

Their readers mostly have no way of testing their claims. Let's face it unless you are able to understand ancient Hebrew, Aramaic and Koine Greek (The languages that the Bible was written in) what chance have you got? It is by reading such books, without informed guidance or anything relating to discernment, that a reader gets taken over by a utopian spirit of expectancy. This in my opinion often leads on to personality disorder.

So obvious is this cloning to me now that whenever I see a TV debate, let's say like 'The Big Question' (BBC1 10am Sundays), when discussing religious matters the Evangelicals are always leading the debate. When I look closely at these evangelicals I see them at various stages of fellowship cloning. I honestly don't mean that to sound as cynical as it does but, unfortunately it has to be said; quite simply in my opinion it is true.

In later chapters I will attempt to discuss how this cloning affects the whole person and forces them to survive their position by using selective use of scripture, the very thing the evangelicals accuse established cults like the Jehovah's Witnesses and the Mormons of.

These days for every one Hal Lindsey there are now another twenty writers expounding on the same theme. These writers present a view of the future that instills a sense of expectancy in the convert. Many (not all) of these fellowships surround themselves with the belief that miracles of healing are commonplace today. This together with the books on prophecy and expected 'Christian behaviour' maps out a way of thinking, a way of life, which stifles lateral thinking and the asking of questions!

When deliverance is promised that doesn't take place the convert/follower is left to try and understand why. This has the effect of leading them deeper into the hijacked mechanics of logic that they need to escape from if they are to attempt to break free.

For the poorly educated and illiterate, this spells out absolute catastrophe, because they are led and encouraged to accept what someone else thinks. Eventually a mindset creeps in with a stilted overview of reality. This leaves the people that accept what they have been taught about how God will determine the future (their future), looking at history and the present through the eyes of an author writing about his claimed insight into biblical prophecy.

Chapter Four

Great Expectations

Human nature is flawed in so many ways. For a former illiterate dreaming his way on to a level playing field, my great human error was to believe in the people that presented 'faith' to me.

It seems very plain to me that Jesus wanted people to believe in Him, not men. We have precisely the opposite happening today. New converts are presented with alpha courses and literature that is written by people who all believe the evangelical position on scripture.

Under the umbrella of religious freedom, we have a marketplace that presents religion in concise, 'clear' packaging. This leaves the door open to the power hungry and those who get turned on by controlling others. What is presented to people in the name of God does not require any proofs. The words of one individual can, through the selective use of scripture, have a devastating effect on people hungry for spiritual reality.

Today we are confronted by a society that is prejudiced against all who do not contribute by providing for themselves. They must work no matter how miserable that work may be! They must put up with total dis-empowerment in the workplace, no unions, and no support of any kind. The almost total ignorance about lower working class suffering is commonplace in our society and has of course spilled over into faith communities of all kinds. The misery that many poorly educated people experience in the workplace is concealed by a skillful use of smoke and mirrors and political indifference, and further confounded by a language of limited definition.

I say this because whenever we get a great number of people unemployed and at the same time other people experiencing misery in their workplace, the casualties of that society start to look for quick convincing answers, anything that can explain away their misery and give them hope for a better tomorrow. If an easy prescriptive 'Answer,' can be provided for people who are under that kind of enormous pressure, it is my sincere belief, based on my own experience, that people will clutch at any straw.

If you have an aching limb and you rub deep heat gel on to it you will get some relief, for a while. Sadly, it does not last and you have to go back to the chemist for more and more. This is where the great expectations are born; these already damaged people are introduced to a future where, it is claimed, anything is possible.

The captivity of the Christian faith by a normalized, capitalist mentality has produced something like a popular DVD/film where the actors are so convincing. To disentangle oneself from this human jungle without real informed help is almost a terminal impossibility. I feel the need to point out that at all times we must guard against spiritual pride. I honestly have no desire to stand in judgment over all the good 'pure in heart' seekers that so often find themselves stifled inside fellowships whose leaders have been deceived by this claustrophobic worldly spirit. However, I also find the 'Judge not lest you be judged' sword of Damocles pointy finger mentality can also be abusive in this situation. If you never talk, dare not talk about what you honestly believe, you will end up with a clockwork God. Surely we all have a right to have the maximum amount of information available to us and to live out our faith to the dictates of our own conscience?

After my first encounter with the evangelical movement, it seemed perfectly natural to assume that this was the model that God was using to carry out His will. This of course was a fatal error. The writings of the ancient biblical scholar, Henry Drummond (1851-1897), give us a great insight into this very human problem. If only, if only he could be here today, then I believe we would have a great presence to aid us through the problems that face the church and fellowship communities.

Drummond outlined the grave consequences of handing over your God-given powers of reasoning to a human organization. One can almost hear him shouting down the years; 'Think for yourself, don't let someone else do the thinking for you'. In his book "Natural Law in the Spiritual World", Henry Drummond takes on the question of spiritual abuse using the word 'parasitism'.

"The form of parasitism exhibited by a certain section of the narrower evangelical school is altogether different from that of the Church of Rome. The parasite in this case seeks its shelter, not in a church, but in a doctrine or a creed... It is put to the individual in the following syllogism: 'you believe Christ died for sinners, you are a sinner therefore Christ died for you; and hence you are saved'. Now what is this but another species of molluscan shell? Could any trap for a benighted soul be more ingeniously planned?"

The ability to activate one's own human reason is something that does not fit well with modern evangelicals. This can easily be explained by the insistence among many evangelicals on having a 'Born again experience'. Other people's 'testimonies' to 'born again experience' surround the seeker. Many become depressed and confused when the penny doesn't drop for them. Expectations are created in the minds of genuine seekers; it is therefore vital that we are aware of the terrible dangers that lurk in the pathways to the subconscious, especially when dealing with vulnerable people.

It is so often the case, particularly in my own experience, that within certain fellowships it is not enough to say, 'I am at peace with God,' No, far from it, one must 'know the word' and 'fit in, have a ministry.'

A cloned copycat behaviour follows. Learning to say 'praise the Lord' at the right time becomes very important amongst other cloned reactions. This leaves poorly educated people in a constant state of dependency on others (eldership elites) and of course open to the worst kind of abuse.

In recent times we have seen the advent of eldership elites - often in large fellowships - that are very difficult to penetrate by reason alone. The dangers here can hardly be overstated. Always, always, top down structures fail the outsider and people from the lower regions of the working class.

I wish I could say that I have found a way forward with this problem; sadly, I remain bewildered by the rejection and indifference that I have experienced, especially among evangelicals.

Present day England is a place where certain activities go on totally unquestioned, 'doing your own thing as long as it doesn't hurt anyone' is the accepted norm. But we all know that blind obedience to something that appears 'right' can threaten one's whole life.

My concern is for all the potential victims of religious abuse. It is my sincere conviction that most if not all religious abuse can be prevented if the right apparatus is in place. This must be born out of a genuine concern for the reputation of the Christian gospel. As I speak the reputation of the gospel in this country is in shreds. The working classes reject what they see. Ever since the days when politicians brought in media management teams to improve their image on T.V. together with glossy publicity leaflets, we have seen a downward spiral in terms of how the average Joe Public views things.

With the advent of large events like 'Spring Harvest' and Christian festivals we have seen the very same management promotional tools used, glossy print outs and magazines with happy smiling faces, people waving hands in the air. We have people saying that this kind of mass event is totally approved by God because, wait for it, it is 'Worship'.

For those who want to point the convinced evangelical finger at me and say; 'Don't judge,' I will hold my hands up and say; "OK guilty, but this is a matter that is far beyond Chris Pitts, beyond all our selfish individualistic salvation; this is about Jesus The Son Of God and how he is being perceived through the eyes of Joe public."

I realize I am walking on to very dangerous ground. If what I am saying has any validity to it then 'WE' as a people, as a 'Church,' have walked into one of the most subtle, Machiavellian, satanic deceptions ever to slime its way into the church. I feel that this personal opinion - (yes, very personal after 43 years personal experience inside many evangelical denominations) - must at least be considered by those who are in leadership roles and someone, someone, has to raise these points. Sadly, the silence continues.

Spring Harvest or Winterheart's Circus?

Of all the deceptions and illusions threatening orthodox Christianity today, I can't think of anything more seducing than the so called 'Christian festivals' or mass Christian events. There exists a mindset behind these events that apparently assumes that if enough people attend and believe the same thing then it must be right? So let us attempt to be a fly on the wall and become invisible observers.

To the sounds of a rock gospel choir singing Shine Jesus Shine still ringing in our ears, I ask the reader to come with me outside the big top crusade tent and accompany me down the road to the town. Come on let's look at the outsiders, please, shall we do that? Do we dare do that?

Here we find the outsider (what some have called the lost). What is Eddie the alcoholic looking for? Is it a professional rock choir with all the thumping fervor of a Glastonbury night? No! It's a reality bigger than the one he is in.

What are the young 'boy racers' looking for as they take out their frustration on the accelerator pedal? Same answer; it's a reality bigger than the one they're in. The elderly racked with pain alone in a twelve by eleven foot flat? The illiterate and poorly educated on the lower, lower regions of working class squalor?

Can these monumental problems really be addressed in a meaningful real way amid the hype, noise and top down structures that hold to a concrete certainty that 'we have got it right' and pursue their repetitions till the genuine seekers get board out of their minds?

Is it any wonder that this country is producing generations of damaged Christians, damaged people, who once had such Great Expectations?

Church attendance may have its place but I feel bound to ask, when is it going to be realized that all the repetitious hymn, prayer, preaching, praise band noise is not going to deliver reality? There are no books, films, meetings that will meet the need of those seeking spiritual reality, a quest I hasten to add that, Chris Pitts is still on.

Chapter Five

A born again Christian in an Edgbaston garden

I will always struggle to find the words that will do justice to the experience of coming out of illiteracy. I like the quote 'A butterfly that escaped the wheel'; however, I remain skeptical that any words exist that can give the reader any real insight. I say this because what should have taken place when I was young and at school was taking place in the mind and body of a 25-year-old man. To put this into perspective, it needs to be pointed out that you don't somehow reach a healthy maturity when you learn to read. The normal life skills that educated people take for granted I was nowhere near possessing. How else can I account for the firm belief that was in my head, that the modern evangelical movement was the only vehicle that God was using to communicate the gospel?

This pious assumption on my part was to lead me into a tangled web of confusion where my mind would be taken over and programmed; I would exhibit egocentric, self-centred, introverted, pretentious, personality altering, dishonest, deceitful, theatrical mimicking, vending machine responses and copycat behaviour. This sick individual that I became, I now must reflect on and it gives me no pleasure at all.

It was in this cesspit of a semi-literate immature brain that I made the fateful decision to study for a diploma at a fundamentalist Bible school situated in a large town in the midlands.

Utterly convinced that this was God's will I took the dreadful decision to ask my wife to give up her job and accompany me. Mary and I moved into a very small room at the Bible school. Although I had a grant it was not enough for two people to exist on so Mary got a job as a SRN at a large hospital. I will never forgive myself for what she went through. What I owe Mary for her constant support and love would fill volumes. The sick plastic-person that I became post evangelical programming leaves me with gut wrenching memories and a self-hatred that is like having to live with a phantom twin.

I tried desperately to fit in with Bible School; however, right from the start we encountered great problems.

It wasn't long before our room was filling up with misfits who just could not cope under the military regime that existed in that place. Together we attempted to help these people. How my wife coped during those times is a matter of utter bewilderment to me now. The fatigue and punishment to her mind and body I am solely responsible for and, dear God, I wish I could go back in time and change every minute! Under the constant shadow of that memory I will confess that what I did, what I became, was sinful and self-indulgent.

Attempting to describe the everyday running of that place is I'm afraid quite simply impossible. I'm left with the choice of trying to describe a time, a world, which is long since gone. An environment so alien, that at this stage in writing this I wonder if it's worth the effort? But I will try.

On arriving at the Bible school with our furniture in my dear friend Anton's van, we were confronted with an ancient property that had a very old fashioned winding staircase. We had to lug our furniture up two flights of stairs where we found a small attic bedsit with no heat, no cooking facilities and a communal toilet on the second floor. Thank God we had an electric fire. This, compared to what some residents were putting up with was 'The Ritz'. We were depressed.

It may have been providential (or good luck?) but the house we moved into had some very strange residents, some of whom were just tenants and not students. One of them was Don Body a lonely desolate man of about forty-five years old. Don had some arrangement with the principal about renting a tiny room, and when I say tiny it was sardine-like in it dimensions. Don's room was next to ours and formed part of the loft conversion. He kept his fridge outside of his room leaning against the banister rails and at times when he opened the fridge door the contents spilled out down three flights of stairs. The inside of Don's room was indescribable; it was stuffed full of old newspapers, discarded tins of baked beans, clothes kept in carrier bags piling up to the ceiling.

Don was a smoker. This proved to be more than dangerous; on more than one occasion he would fall asleep, the newspaper would ignite and smoke would billow out under his door. Quite honestly living anywhere near Don was purgatory. Our very lives were in danger many times.

Another resident Mr. Cooper rented a room on the second floor; he was a frail eighty-year-old man with a mild personality disorder, a very lonely man. It didn't take much to upset Mr. Cooper. For some unfathomable reason the principal of the school had allowed a Chinese student a Mr. David Loo to have a room very near to Mr. Cooper. Mr. Loo would constantly freak Mr. Cooper out. Mr. Cooper was certain that Mr. Loo was observing 'strange rituals' with a sword that Mr. Loo kept in his room.

The other student on the ground floor Tony was a very quiet man. Tony was 'head of house' (that apparently meant that he had to report people that did not make the 5.30 am prayer meeting). Tony and his wife were two of the most quiet people I've ever come across. Thank God they were not natural informers and never grassed on us when we did not get up in time for the early morning prayer meeting!

The morning assembly took place at about 9am. A very strict, somber affair.

Wearing traditional long black clothes the Principal, followed by the Vice Principal and lecturers, would process in to the meeting hall, at which point all the students would have to stand up as a mark of respect. It was literally like the film 'Goodbye Mr. Chips' on constant replay.

The daily routine was 5-30am: students rise for prayer meeting. After this, if it did not clash with lectures we were allowed to skip assembly and then to go out onto the streets of the town and preach the gospel. All students were assigned a 'Commando Team' with a captain!

Commando Teams. The very name should convey to the reader that this was something bizarrely awful. And my God it was!

Many students already fatigued by lack of sleep stumbled their way onto the streets. This was an experience that has scarred me. It was confrontational, unnecessary, and at times just plain stupid. It was as if the school was purposely trying to go back to the time of Wesley. There were countless other ways to communicate with people but we appeared to be stuck in some kind of historical drama.

Chores. In the afternoons students were expected to carry out 'Chores'. This strange use of an American word was to describe the students being expected to carry out everything from roof repairs, to cleaning and in my case, gardening.

What I am about to describe is one of the most excruciating emotionally painful experiences of my entire life. During my first experience of carrying out chores I learned that a student had fallen off the roof of one of the lecture blocks. The school had expected him to repair the failing roof and while attempting this repair he had fallen and broken his back. This condemned him to being in a wheelchair for the rest of his life and his poor wife to being his carer. Of course the usual hype was generated about him 'being healed if we have enough faith'; however, this incident happened in the mid 70's, and last time I checked this out with a former student (approximately four years ago) he is still in a wheelchair, God help him.

I include this account firstly because evangelical programming leaves you believing that 'Born again experience' cannot be questioned; it is something that God himself has brought about in a convert to the faith! Secondly, to leave an account of how the destruction of a young vulnerable mind and personality can take place in a closed, very well-protected, abusive, controlling, environment.

God forgive those involved. I think I have, but really, only God knows if I really have, doesn't He?

At that time, however naïve it may sound, I was utterly convinced that all 'Born again' Christians had the Holy Spirit ruling their life and were good loving people. What I was about to find out, experience first hand, was for me like having a corkscrew inserted into my heart!

I was soon given my chores to carry out; I was to work in the garden of a Pentecostal minister and his wife. How these people were able to get a young student to do their garden remains an open question, but they did.

I could never make out whether these people were students or residents. I was expected to tend a large area at the rear of their house. This meant digging the soil over and weeding. This went on OK for a while; however, one day I was weeding an area where some plants had been laid. I must have mistaken a plant for a weed and hoed it up. The Pentecostal minister's wife came out of the house to inspect my work. She was a woman of about 30 years old. When she noticed the mistake I'd made in removing a plant that I mistook for a weed, she let out a tirade of verbal abuse at me, the like of which I had not known before, or since. So aggressive was this that I literally shook. It was as if the ground was swallowing me up. She was out of control, totally, out of control. I was traumatized and feeling sick, why? Because at that very moment I knew, I just knew that I HAD BEEN DECEIVED.

Soon after this incident I saw this very same woman at an evening meeting with her hands held high in the air, a radiant smile on her face supposedly 'Praising God'.

Words fail me here but, even now after all these years I can hear the words of the young Bob Dylan ringing in my ears. I can't recall exactly what I heard on that day, all I can say is I hope it was these great descriptive words:

"The rules of the road have been lodged, it's only people's games that you've got to dodge. From fixtures and forces and friends your sorrow does stem, they'll hype you and type you making you feel that you got to be just like them. It is not he, she, them or it that you belong to."

I don't remember walking back to the attic room; I don't know how long it took me; all I knew in my heart and soul was that IT WAS OVER. Something final and irrevocable had taken place, I yearned for my former freedom, but I did not realize the shattered brokenness I was in. It was to take many years to repair; has it ever repaired? The only honest answer, I think, is no! I don't think it will ever really leave me. And what of the thousands of my fellow travelers who went through similar or worse experiences, what of them? What of them? They have simply disappeared.

I have headed this chapter 'A born again Christian in an Edgbaston garden' The term 'Born again Christian' is as bankrupt as the day it was invented. It has become the easy target of new age comedians. The working class sneer at its absurdities as they see nice rich 'Born again' people show up to churches in their B.M.Ws and twenty thousand pound cars. Frank Zapper once wrote; 'Brown shoes don't make it' and in my opinion, nor does, 'A born again Christian in an Edgbaston garden', but sadly the circus goes on.

Chapter Six

God save us from what we become

Everyone's pain is uniquely personal. The people that I knew back then all had their personal hells. Having to become something 'special' is very draining on the mind and body. Ships have anchors but we only had sails, or it would be more correct to say, supposed Spirit sails.

One of the hardest things to describe is when you are told that you will experience, this, that, and the other, by people you believe divinely appointed to guide you, and then, you do not experience that thing. The effect on the human psyche can be very dangerous.

If you believe that you are in a safe environment and that God Himself has led you, then the potential for cloning and abuse is ever present. It's like a form of adoption; your substitute parents are 'God given' and absolutely trustworthy. This type of abuse is anti-Christian, and one wonders where it is coming from? According to the logic I assume here, it can only come from three places, God, Satan, or human delusion.

Only those who have direct experience of this know the full extent of that lonely desolate human misery. For example as a direct result of that cloning I actually lied to myself and other people. I would say that I had witnessed healing that had never taken place, in some twisted belief that if I said it had happened, it would happen!

This cloning abuse was both mental and physical. For me the guilt that I carried caused me to become sick in body and mind. I would suffer migraine after migraine. The results of this assault on my personality mere words cannot describe. I became a sub–human vending machine. There seems to be an assumption in this new–age version of 'Christianity' that if a large number of people all say the same thing, think the same thing, act the same thing, then it must be true. I am living proof that it is not.

Today the ongoing evolution of this goes something like this: 'I feel safe in the crowd and at home here; God himself must want me here.' This mentality assumes cast iron certainties about belief and behaviour in the minds of vulnerable people; its dangers can hardly be overstated.

When we look at the kind of activity that goes on at large Christian gatherings like Spring Harvest and other similar events, what do we see? A vast amount of books are on sale all written by well-educated people all supporting the evangelical position on scripture, church activity, and expected behaviour. (N.B. This has nothing to do with accepting the Bible as an inspired document I'm talking about a stilted overview of scripture).

CD's are on sale by 'Christian artists' and rock bands whose commercial intensity rivals that of the secular music industry. Christian radio stations are popping up all over this country to support these activities; followers are compelled to accept all this activity as the Christian norm.

Despite what you may hear about these radio stations, the only people they are interested in are the people who all agree with the general evangelical overview of scripture and society. This, as I have stated before, can be extremely limited. The same may be said of other big festival events. Where is the place for the outsider, those who question and dare to ask; 'Does all this really relate to Jesus of Nazareth?'

When I have tried to engage the organizers of these events in conversation, I have come across a mountain of bureaucracy and indifference. Once at Spring Harvest I met a lovely man who appeared to listen to me, but I fear he encountered great problems when he took my concerns to a higher level. The brain—police are everywhere; this does not inspire me with confidence, especially, where there are young people, who are full of good will, vitality and hope. What happened to my friends and myself can and will happen again.

As I reflect on the vast labyrinth of the past so

many voices echo along those time tunnels. "Make the dream live" I hear one Pastor shouting. "Whose dream?" I now ask. Our dreams are either limited or expanded by our life experience. A person from a middle class background, whose family is reasonably well off, will have a dream that reflects that experience. If they have never seen the inside of a long stay ward in a psychiatric hospital or geriatric unit they will know nothing of the wretchedness there. Their dream will be limited and confined. Is their dream God's dream? NO, NO, NO. So God is shrunk into an idol of a person's hopes and aspirations. Very, very individualistic — person-centered. I feel like screaming at this point, 'Christ came for the whole world!' But I don't have to scream, because, if my faith is true, then God is already screaming in the silence.

After this I reflect on the hungry souls from deprived areas of existence. Some have seen fit to describe these people as 'working class.' I will try to argue that this does not come anywhere near describing their personal circumstances. Their dreams can possibly be identified with God's will; St Paul writes, "For God has chosen the base things of this world which are despised," people whom this present society has turned its back on. When the 'iron lady' banished them to the wastelands of (in her and her followers' minds) the undeserving poor, their dis-empowerment was to become terminal.

I would like to identify all those mentioned above who are invisible to human eyes but hopefully very present in God's. Some are slipping into noisy fellowships looking for hope; they slip out very quickly too. These people, don't let them fool you; they can discern if there is love for them in any given place! The one thing they do have is a God given discernment, something that a degree in theology will never give you. What are the 'Fellowships,' 'Churches,' doing about the dreams of those damaged people who cannot articulate their hopes and aspirations? The truth is they don't even know they exist. A diabolical ignorance exists in a world of theatre and noise.

If present day society reflects the world's priorities, then the church should reflect God's priorities. I have heard so many excuses, but in the end it's the same old song. There is a clear threshold beyond which the modern church does not wish to reason. There are so many 'Church goers' bored out of their minds by repetitious, set in stone, activity. There are terrible dangers here. If the road to Hell is paved with good intentions then what chance do people have who have been schooled on; "Do not rebuke an elder!" 'You must just keep quiet and pray!' Isaiah chapter fifty-eight verse seven speaks of 'the poor who are cast out.' This is sometimes very cleverly done; certain types of religious mentality can justify anything.

You can be so certain that your church is doing the right thing that you miss seeing what it doesn't do; sometimes church going can be very delusional. The street was the place where Jesus took on the hard-core realities of this world. Modern day religion takes place behind closed doors.

Even those church/fellowships that now have 'Street Pastors' can have an agenda very different to 'Loving your neighbor as yourself''.

Within this broken body, trust in men is easy, trust in God is a lot more expensive. God save us from what we become; God forgive me for what I became. Self-hatred is a crippling thing; God may forgive me, but I don't feel much like forgiving myself. If you feel 'safe' and 'secure' in a large fellowship or church, think very hard about what you are involved with.

My cast iron certainties left me with a personality disorder that eventually threatened my marriage and led me back into the most vile sin. I worshipped my own conclusions, salvation was 'I, ME, Mine' – self-centered. Sometimes I doubt whether I ever really believed in Jesus of Nazareth the Son of God.

Chapter Seven

Crossing the party line

Lumps in the soup

For some the Christian faith is a set meal you can rely on. There are never any lumps in the soup. Try to start a discussion with a regular church-goer about where we fail. Among the responses I've received are: 'in our church we don't have problems like that!' Immediately they go on the defensive. If Christ had words for the seven churches in the book of Revelation what would he think of the present day? Sometimes he praised a church, sometimes he had harsh words; can we possibly believe that he would have an agreeable smile on His face when He looks at present day churches?

I fear there can be grave self-delusion in modern day fellowships unless this is faced head on.

In politics if an M.P. is not toeing the party line he is put under pressure by 'the whips'. The Christian faith is not meant to be a political party. When Margaret Thatcher became prime–minister she quoted from the prayer of St Francis. If ever there was an example of betrayal you have it there! "Where there is despair let us bring hope,' what a sick statement that was. Under the guise of serving some great political purpose millions of people from the lower working class were consigned to the scrap heap.

Thousands of evangelical Christians supported Thatcher's government. Her special relationship with the U.S. government of the day puts into perspective her attitude to the working poor and the unemployed of those times. You may not be able to see 'The Whips' in your church or fellowship but they are always, always there.

The grave self–delusion and smug self-assurance that possessed me has a very powerful spirit behind it. If I am speaking to someone reading this I would simply ask:

1) When you are totally alone, away from all the hype and noise, are you really, really at peace?
2) Do you feel the need to live up to someone else's experience?
3) Is there an aching hunger that mere fellowship attendance does not satisfy?

It was these questions and more that led me to cross the party line. I left and walked away from all of it. I just knew that I had to do this.

I was now in a place where every pastor, priest or elder that I had ever known would condemn me. I was outside of everything that I once believed to be safe. I knew full well that I would be accused of 'looking for a perfect church!' 'He is very judgmental'. As far as people like that were concerned I had lost my faith. Well, there is some truth in that! I went through years of lonely hopeless wandering and yes; I did become alcohol dependent amongst a lot more squalor.

Confused by the tangled processing and cloning that I had undergone, I had to find Chris Pitts again before I could start to think again.

My wife Mary just loved me sacrificially through it all and again bore the brunt of my suicidal depression.

The way I look at it now is like this; if God is real, He will find me. I look to no man, no worldly organization. I think for the first time I'm in with a chance!

One of the first things I did was to fraternize with the other side; I went to the Catholic Church. I spent a long time talking with Catholics, priests and laity. At first the guilt was heavy upon me; however, I found a peace among some catholic charismatics. It was just so different to the world I knew. There was an ordinary everyday thing about these people that I liked a lot. If you could separate history from the present day catholic church it would be a good cul-de-sac resting place for former evangelicals. This is no place to debate theology or church history anyway; in the end I honestly don't believe that God cares about denominational boundaries. During all my searching, all my depression I never lost contact with the uniqueness of Christ. There were some who said I would end up on the primrose path to liberal theology, IT DID NOT HAPPEN. Some said; 'Chris will come back to the Lord some day.' I now respond; 'How can I come back to something I never really went away from?' I came away from religious power abuse, nothing else.

The set menu has changed. I'm now a vegetarian.

Crossing the party line will be one of the most desolate lonely things you ever do. For me it literally pushed me to the edge. It will amaze you when you see the unnecessary baggage we carry; however there's no gain without pain here.

I now look back in stark amazement at the badges and luggage that my fellow 'Christians' put on me. I have been told by some (I think) trustworthy friends that if you want to get close to 'The Jesus of history, The Christ of faith' prepare for the loneliest walk of your life. I'm not there yet, nowhere near!

In attempting to describe the tangled web of deception that has entered the Church and Christian communities (descriptions here tend to be vague) treading on toes is I'm afraid an occupational hazard.

An individual's behaviour is conditioned by what we think is 'normal'. It is here again that I want to ask questions:

1) Is it accepted as 'normal' that 'Christians' have ambitions and work for reward in a capitalist

society? If it is, how can anyone 'surrender to Christ'?

2) As that society has normalized the 'unacceptable face of capitalism' surely it is impossible to reconcile this in any way to the life of Christ?

3) If we have a Church that sees the ownership of property, investment, and has an internal organizational inner structure that imitates the world, then are we not attempting to start from an impossible position?

It is at this point that I invite all who are dissatisfied and bored to death with the mind-games of ritualistic fellowship/church attendance to cross the party line.

You/we simply have no choice. Procrastination is pointless.

If knowing all this we simply get up and go to work tomorrow into a workplace that normalizes lying, fighting for position, status and personal-power, what the hell is the point?

I see this as the root of all the problems paralyzing the Christian faith.

If (according to St Paul) one part of the body is suffering then we all suffer. That truth can never fight its way through to what we dare to call 'Church' today.

We don't need buildings. We don't need investments. We don't need hernia of the eardrum 'Praise Bands'. We don't need large screen projection. We don't need magazines. We need Jesus Christ. He crossed the line a long time ago and is waiting for us to follow.

Chapter Eight

Dancing with a crippled giant

I can't help but think that thousands of good sincere Christians have ended up on the scrap heap because they have been fed a false expectation based on selective use of scripture.

Many poorly educated and vulnerable people give their heart and soul to fellowships that simply claim 'we are the one true way to go, we know this because Jesus has told us!' The vulnerable, sick, depressed, lonely, gullible, weak, poor, are left to fester in these mausoleums of delusion.

I would venture to claim that these victims are in Christ's own words 'In prison' and no one is visiting them. This is in my opinion sinful and wicked and will eventually undermine what is left of the Christian witness in this country.

There is, in human nature the need for a spiritual life. However in this country genuine seekers are being left to wander in dangerous spiritual supermarkets with no guidebook. The simple fact that this is happening is enough to show the total indifference of most 'Church fellowships' to the problem of abuse.

I don't believe that God wants walking-vending machines, clones that leave the victims helpless, riddled with guilt, believing that if they leave a fellowship they are going against God's will, programmed products of demonstrative environments. I believe He wants real people with all the human failings, frailties and absurdities that are common to our race. People who know there is no side to be on, nothing to protect, nothing to prove!

So we must look at the New Testament and history and seek out as much information as we can. Can we be guided to a safe spiritual place? How can we be sure that we are on 'Safe Ground'? How do we recognize the work of the Holy Spirit?

Anyone who is a member of the Christian faith will believe that the Holy Spirit is at work all the time in ways far past human understanding, but I want to ask Is there any evidence that the Holy Spirit is at work in these questionable 'Fellowships' in the way that they claim?

a) Exclusive to their application of 'The Gospel' and
b) Their view of scripture?
c) If I had a penny for all the times a person has said to me, "The Lord told me!" I would be a very rich man.

Some evangelicals believe that the very same gifts of healing that Christ and the apostles manifested are in operation today, others take a contrary view.

Calvinist and Armenian separate from each other. All claim the leading of the Spirit!

When we consider this question the first thing to appreciate is that individual people can achieve great acts of service within any kind of fellowship. This will be seen as inspired by the love of God in Christ. However, the concept of the Holy Spirit sanctioning one view of Holy Scripture is a vexed and complicated one. There is then the far more complicated question of what people perceive the work of the Holy Spirit to be.

We can only try and answer this by looking at the life of Christ in its entirety not selectively. Speaking for myself, the best example of the work of the Holy Spirit I can think of is a place where you get such an outpouring of love, that outside people say; 'We want what you have got'. Repenting of sin is then seen as a consequence of experiencing the pure unadulterated love of God.

This love causes people of diverse backgrounds to reach out to each other. The bank manager will reach out to the road sweeper and a silent revolution will come. A revelation will come.

If Paul and Barnabas had disagreements then we should not look for doctrinal perfection. The early church was just as human as the churches of today. Christ said, 'by your love will all men know that you are my disciples'.

Anyone who has known Christians who have experienced denominational abuse will know the urgency to address these problems. In this world the only side to be on is the one that loves the most. This, in my opinion, was 'once and for all' perfected in the life of Christ.

Where God is and who's side He is on will be argued out in a very, very uncertain future. All I have done is to try and point out to the bewildered traveler, seeker, potential victim, some personal observations from a road, my road, that looks back on a forty-year history among evangelicals; some good, some bad, some ugly.

"But I can't think for you you'll have to decide, whether Judas Iscariot had God on his side."

Chapter Nine

Towards the beginnings of an answer

If we know there is a problem and do nothing then we do not deserve the word 'Christian' to be addressed to us. Better one step at a time than to do nothing. Militant atheistic humanism is on the march and sooner or later they will start 'Christian de-programming'.

The cost of procrastination will be measured in the loss of any real Christian witness to this country. The average 'Joe in the street' will take note of programmed personalities bent out of shape by rogue fellowships (also activity regarded as normal in some established charismatic churches) and regard Christians as 'nutters'. (Or words I cannot use here).

In all my experience among the Evangelicals I have never known a minister, pastor or leader who really wants to engage with the lower, lower regions of the working class. Whether it is because of ignorance fear or strategic evasion I don't know, but I am absolutely sure as I write this that the unknown, unseen, unreported area of human existence I have described in former chapters is a growing reality. The lack of response in this area would be bewildering were it not for the obvious British mentality behind top down structures. Alongside this is the failure to recognize that 'educated elites' are always structured to fail when it comes to reaching out to the dispossessed and dis-empowered. The spiritual pride that comes out of the mouths of 'Christians' in this area is sickening - statements like

'I really understand THESE PEOPLE!'

'But you know sometimes they are the hardest people to help!'

'They just won't help themselves!'

This impasse, this terminal stubbornness inherent in the cast iron certainties of modern evangelical mindsets has proved to be the final straw that broke the camel's back for me. It is here that a cataclysmic atomic blasting has left me with no choice but to turn my back permanently, irrevocably on the modern evangelical movement. During this essay I have come back to the words of the young Bob Dylan many times; he seemed to have an X-ray insight at one point in his life. I believe he allowed his listeners to share that, but that was long, long ago before they put a tax on happiness!

These days I may be groping in the dark trying to find something in the ruins of a once evangelical baptized faith but at least I fear none of the crowd-pullers and their paramilitaries. I take great comfort in the words of the young Bob Dylan that speaks of my post programmed state:

"I'll tell it and speak it and think it and breathe it, and reflect from the mountains so all souls can see it and I'll stand on the ocean until I start sinking but I'll know my song well before I start singing."

Forty years of anyone's life is surely enough time to know the song?

Throughout this essay there has been one recurring theme, namely the abuse of power. When authority is in the hands of individuals who believe that they are serving a great purpose, in this case the greatest of all purposes, the will of God, then they must be accountable. If a whole generation of damaged people is pushed out of our thinking by the stroke of a pen, I believe that is sinful and wicked. In writing this I have become increasingly aware of just how unpopular this subject is among evangelicals. Human nature must take its share of the blame. People promoted to a level of incompetence must share that blame too.

I want so much to see the prison door opened for the spiritually abused; however I have no reason to hope at this point. I certainly do not wish the Hard Rain that Dylan was singing about all those years ago to fall on the Evangelicals. I am however assured, that unless some real honest internal examination of this out of control beast is undertaken then indeed a very hard rain will fall.

Christian radio stations and the God Channel give a legitimacy to a vast labyrinth network that worships its own conclusions and shuts out dissenters (especially people like myself who dare to contact them on their 'phone-in chat shows') and anyway their absolute conviction that they are right leaves me believing that they couldn't see the point if it was needle sharp and they were sitting on it. Against this vast tapestry of indifference I walk away.

Sadly since writing this small essay I have become agnostic on just about everything. I look forward to a time when I can look at a Suffolk sunset and see God in it as I once did; yes, I am waiting. I salute all my fellow victims, people who never did anything to hurt anyone, tossed on the slag heap of a crass indifference to suffer alone, while Mr. Crowd-Puller and his acolytes proclaim that their lives have meaning, skillfully articulating a middle class gospel of limited definition, carrying in his left hand a large bucket of whitewash and in his right hand the testimonials from a cloistered academia, with the brilliant well-trained tongue moving to a perfect exhaling of convincing word-power but, disguising the stench of a Machiavellian evasiveness that can only be smelt by an emperor who has, for once, really got all his clothes on.

I bid goodbye to the Idols and twisted conclusions of the modern evangelical. I go my way with the burden of knowing that an unknown number of damaged people are out there somewhere, victims of a system that can dish out cast iron certainties and doctrinal perfection, but knows nothing of mercy to those it has left abandoned/ helpless and alone.

-oOo-

Postscript

It is almost impossible to describe the hopelessness that I feel as I look upon the future of anything that is called 'Christian'. However, this is my hopelessness and I do not wish to leave the impression that anything I have written here is saying that the Christian faith is untrue or unworthy of investigation. I simply say beware of those who offer you cast iron certainties and healing, particularly if they look the picture of health and are wearing a smile.

'When I get up in the morning, the first thing I do is smile, I like to get it over with!'

W.C. Fields

About the Author

Chris Pitts, songwriter, poet, activist and advocate for the elderly lives at Nayland, Colchester in Essex with his wife Mary. His websites are chrispitts.co.uk and chrispitts-music.com.

Printed in Great Britain
by Amazon